Fun with
AESOP
Reader

Retold by Paul Tell

Illustrated by Connie Ross

Fun with
AESOP
Reader

Retold by Paul Tell

Illustrated by Connie Ross

TELCRAFT ®

For readers & listeners
of all ages

Many thanks to those who helped bring the
original *Fun With Aesop* 3-volume set into
print, with special thanks to Dianna Williams,
Marti Geise, and Jim Coleman for their
editorial work bringing the stories together into
a single volume. The same excellent storybook
illustrations by Connie Ross remain, and with
pleasure this edition is presented for both
reader and listener to enjoy.

TELCRAFT®
A Division of Tell Publications
Mogadore, Ohio 44260

© 1991 by Tell Publications, All Rights Reserved
Published in Mogadore, Ohio, by Tell Publications
Manufactured in the United States of America
Library of Congress Catalog Card Number 91-90956
ISBN 1-878893-04-1 Trade Paper
ISBN 1-878893-05-X Trade Hardcover
ISBN 1-878893-10-6 Library Binding

The paper in this book meets the guidelines for
permanence and durability of the Committee on
Production Guidelines for Book Longevity of the
Council on Library Resources. ∞

Contents

About this book

Fun with Aesop Reader presents timeless ideas that Aesop, a Greek slave, told as fables during the 6th century B.C.

This book developed as the fables were read to children ages 4 - 6, and as they were read aloud by those ages 7 - 10.

Each fable includes a question with an answer, and ends with a rhythmic retelling that returns the reader to the beginning in a more personal way, like the memories of life often do.

The stories don't grow old—they grow more interesting as they are read again and again. Their themes, their characters are found in many places, sometimes when they are least expected, crossing differences in interest, wealth, education, and culture.

Paul Tell is experienced in leading small groups. Avoiding lecture, he uses questions to encourage participation and group discovery. The Aesop story question, with answer page, are for the reader to think about, to possibly question or apply more specifically. Earning an M.A. in Mass Media Communication, the author combines a business background with love of teaching, encouraging lifelong learning beyond formal education. He is father of three boys, themselves now grown with families of their own. He especially enjoys writing while out-of-doors.

Part I

The Rabbit and the Turtle

Sammy Rabbit was a runner. Lickety-split he'd dash from place to place.

"Sometimes I see a streak of gray and white from the corner of my eye," said Mr. Beaver to his wife.

"It's Sam Rabbit, I know!" said Mrs. Beaver. "I have seen it too, and when I look up he's already gone."

Sammy smiled when he heard them talk like this.

One day when the animals were gathered together, Sammy said to them, "I challenge anyone here to race with me."

Everyone grew quiet.

Then from way in the back a voice broke the silence:

"I accept your challenge."

The animals quickly turned to look. Much to their surprise they saw it was Jimmy Turtle speaking!

Now Sammy thought this was silly and laughed until he rolled on the ground. "What an easy race to win," he snickered.

Then getting up on one elbow, Sammy said, "I can't believe YOU would want to race. Why, I could run circles around you all the way, and still win!"

Now Jimmy was serious about racing. Looking Sammy right in the eye he said, "Wait 'til you've won before you say any more."

The other animals soon set up a running path.

At the starting line, Sammy wore a great big smile as he looked all around. But Jimmy kept looking straight ahead.

As Mr. Otter began the starting call, Sammy leaned back, ready to spring forward. Jimmy was quite different, standing low to the ground on all four feet. He didn't look much higher (or faster) than a rock with a flat bottom.

"Ready, set . . . GO!"
And the race began.

At the sound of "GO," dust flew everywhere as Sammy darted out ahead. Soon he was out of sight. The cloud began to settle and there walked Jimmy. It looked as though he'd hardly started!

After a while Sammy stopped. He felt good as he looked ahead and could see where the race would end.

Thinking he had plenty of time, Sammy decided to lie down for a nap on the soft, cool grass under a tree.

Jimmy never stopped. He just kept walking on his short, flat feet with a thump . . . thump . . . thump.

Sometimes the bottom of his shell would bump the ground as he stepped into a hole or crawled over the root of a tree. But with his neck stretched out, he just kept walking, going on . . . and on, and on.

Later, Sammy woke up, rubbed his eyes and blinked, not knowing how long he had been asleep.

Suddenly, his eyes opened wide. No! There was Jimmy, about to cross the finish line!

Every muscle in Sammy wanted to jump up and run. But it was too late. Sammy was too far behind to catch up with that turtle and win.

He stood frozen as he watched Jimmy finish with a thump . . . thump . . . thump.

Someone heard Jimmy say something as he crossed the line.

What do you think he said?

*Slow and steady
wins the race.*

The important thing
is not
How *fast* you run.
It's *not stopping*
until you *finish*.

To do a job,
just get started and
Keep going, keep going,
and soon you
will be done.

Rabbits like to run—
   to play. Their feet
Are fast and fur is soft;
   what fun to
     see them run!

Turtles are nice
   in a different way.
Determined—they
   walk with stiffened steps
     and sway from side to side.

Rabbits dart
   when danger comes,
But a turtle tucks
   inside his shell and waits
     'til danger's passed.

Rabbits are fun
   to touch if you can;
While turtles are simply there,
   looking good at rest
     by a quiet pond.

You may be quick like a rabbit
   and maybe a little cute;
But don't forget, there are
   times to be like a turtle.
     Listen, it's true:

Steady walking
   beats running
And stopping,
   running
     and stopping.

The Crow and the Pitcher

What a hot, dry day, thought Johnny Crow. I think I'll die if I don't get something to drink!

Then Johnny saw a pitcher. It was standing near a well. He jumped up hopefully and stood on its brim. Looking down into it, he saw some water at the bottom.

You could almost hear him thinking: How wonderful that water looks. I must have some. I really must!

But try as he might, Johnny couldn't lean in far enough to reach the water. And all the while he was getting more and more thirsty!

He wasn't strong enough to tip the pitcher, and if he jumped inside he might not be able to fly back out. He thought and thought until he had a plan.

Then he jumped to the ground and picked up a pebble in his beak. He hopped back up and dropped it into the pitcher. He did this again and again, keeping his eye on the water.

He saw the water coming up little by little with every pebble he dropped. Good, he thought, but it's still too far down to reach.

I know what I'll do. I'll keep on dropping in pebbles, more and more of them.

At last, after Johnny had filled the pitcher with many pebbles, the water came up high enough to reach.

Happily he drank until he was full!

How did Johnny get what he needed?

Johnny thought of a good idea,
  then,

Little by little,
    without stopping,
      he reached his goal.

Was Johnny's good idea,
  by itself,
    enough to get the water?

Think about it:
First,
    Johnny *thought* of a good idea.
Then,
    he *started doing it.*
And,
    kept on doing it until finally he
      could reach the water.

      It's as simple as that.
        Think of an idea.
        Start doing it,
        And keep on doing it
            until it's done.

18

Mr. Crow,
   you cock your head
     and look.
What are you thinking?
   What do you want?
     I'd really like to know.

Water!
   Just the thought of it
     makes me thirsty.
My mouth is so dry;
   my tongue feels
     like stone.
The sun is hot today
   and the road very dusty.
 The trees are fortunate;
   they drink from far below.
Water, water,
   I must have some—
     I'm so thirsty!

There's a well, and a pitcher,
   an old glass pitcher
On the stones by the side
   of the well.
I'll take a look.
   Maybe someone left
     a little to drink.
Ooooh—I see some water,
   but I can't lean down
     far enough to reach it.
I know what I'll do.
   I'll drop in some pebbles—
Carry them in my beak,
   one at a time.
I see the water rising,
   very slowly.
With each pebble I drop,
   it gets a little higher!
Now I can reach it!
   What cool, clear water.
I'll throw my head back,
   let it trickle right down!

19

A Bell for the Cat

A family of mice lived in a big house with a very sly cat.

One day the mice held a meeting. "What can we do to protect ourselves from the cat?" they asked each other.

They talked, and after a while agreed that their biggest problem was the way the cat would quietly sneak up on them.

They decided they needed to know when the cat was coming. But HOW could they be warned?

It was quiet for a while as they tried to think of an idea.

"I've got it!" young Jeremy Mouse cried out. "I know what will warn us whenever the cat is coming!"

Jeremy had everyone's attention. Then lowering his voice, he told them his idea, as if he were letting them in on a secret. "Our warning," he said, "will be the sound of a bell!"

"A bell?" questioned the others.

"Yes, a BELL. I propose we tie a bell on a ribbon around the cat's neck. Whenever we hear the bell, we can run and hide until he has gone!"

"Hooray!" The mice cheered and clapped loudly. They thought this was a great idea, until . . .

Mr. Bishop, a very old mouse, stood up and raised his hand. Everyone became very quiet, more quiet than when young Jeremy was telling his idea.

Mr. Bishop had seen and thought about many things. In a voice just above a whisper, he spoke. "This all sounds very interesting, but WHO will tie the bell around the cat's neck?"

What can you learn from Jeremy and Mr. Bishop?

It's easy to think of ideas
you cannot do.

Now, once you learn *this* lesson,
quickly learn another:

Try to be wise like Mr. Bishop,
but also keep thinking
of new ideas like Jeremy!

It's true that not every idea will
work. But don't stop thinking of
new ideas and don't worry about
suggesting one that won't work.
Some of the best plans start with
an impossible idea that is changed
a little into a plan that will work.

Bells for kittens—
   it's a great idea;
Every cat
   should have one.

A bell for babies
   and their mothers
And their
   fathers too.

Yes, A BELL
   FOR ALL CATS,
The greatest idea
   yet.

Hooray for the
   well-being
Of all
   concerned mice.

Now at our house,
   we'll just take
A ribbon with a bell
   and tie it around the neck
      of that very sly cat!

Then we'll hear him coming
   every time.
We'll hear him coming
   and we'll run and hide
      until he has gone.

Yes, a great idea,
   a great idea!
But WHO, please tell me
   WHO will tie the bell
      to this cat?

The Bundle of Sticks

One day a father lay sick in bed. He thought about the things he wanted his children to know.

There was one important lesson he wanted them to learn. So he called them to his bedside.

He asked the oldest to go and bring back some sticks, one for each of them, and a string.

Wondering what their father would show them, the children waited until the oldest returned. Then, they watched their father take the sticks, count them, and tie them into a bundle.

Starting with the youngest, he asked her to take the bundle and see if she could break it. She tried with all her might but the sticks wouldn't break.

The father then asked the others to
take a turn to see who might break the
bundle. They all tried, but none of them
could break it, not even the oldest.

As they looked at each other and at the
bundle, the father told the oldest to untie
the sticks, give one to each of his brothers
and sisters, and keep the last stick for
himself.

"Now," said their father, "try to break
them!"

Suddenly, the air filled with a crackling
sound as all the sticks broke. Even the
youngest was able to break her stick.

"Do you know the lesson this teaches?"
asked their father.

What do you think their father was
trying to teach them?

Together you are strong;
Separated you are weak.

There's an old saying
to remember:

United we stand,
divided we fall.

United means "together."
Divided means "separated."

Stay together, help each other,
and you'll be your strongest.

26

Sticks,
   just sticks.
One by one
   you can break them.

Together?
   No. They won't break
When they're
   together!

But just separate them
   and see
How easily
   they will break!

So if you want to
   keep them strong,
Just put them all together;
Then whatever happens,
   they won't break.

The Donkey and the
Lion's Skin

Once upon a time a donkey found a lion's skin which hunters had hung to dry in the sun.

"How exciting it would be to dress up and look like a lion!" said the donkey. Soon he was under the lion's skin and pulled it down over him.

As he walked toward the village everyone was afraid and started to run.

"What fun!" cried the donkey.

Feeling very proud of himself,
the donkey lifted his head and let out
a loud bra-a-a-ay.

Now this is not the sound that lions
make, only donkeys!

A fox quickly turned back toward the
donkey and said, "I know you by your
voice."

What does this story tell us about
trying to fool someone?

Clothes may disguise us,
but when we talk,
Others will know who we
really are.

A person who dresses up like
someone else will soon be
discovered for who he really is
when he begins to talk!

Donkeys see
  and donkeys do;
Yes, donkeys act
  as donkeys will.

Tell me to walk
  and I'll stand still;
Tell me to stand
  and off I'll go.

A lion's skin—
  how perfect
To make me into
  a kingly beast.

There, I've got it on!
  How great it feels,
And look how the
  others run!

I'm very important,
  strong and brave.
I'll raise my voice,
  make the others shake.

Bra-a-a-ay!
  Bra-a-a-a-a-ay!
Oops! Now
  what have I done?

Oh, oh, my secret's out—
  first the fox,
Now all the others know
  I'm really a donkey!

The Fox and the Grapes

One day a fox was walking through the woods. He saw some grapes hanging from a vine over a tree limb, and his mouth began to water.

The grapes looked so good that he decided he must have some.

He jumped and jumped, springing up as high as he could. But try as he might, he couldn't jump high enough to reach them.

He quickly looked around to make
sure that no one was watching. No fox
will admit he cannot do something.

In a final, desperate attempt, the fox
started from way back and ran full speed
to a new jumping spot. As he reached it
he leaped into the air with all his might.

This time he came closer to the grapes,
but still not close enough to snatch even
one!

Disappointed, he looked around once
more just to be sure no one had seen
him trying to reach the grapes. Then he
walked away saying something to himself.

What do you think he said?

*I really didn't want
those grapes.
They must be very sour!*

Question:
Do you think
the grapes were sour?

The fox acted like people sometimes act:
If a person can't have something
he wants, he may SAY he really
doesn't want it—he may even say
something is WRONG with it,
as if he did not want it at all.

34

Grapes
   so purple,
Juicy,
   good.

They look so round, so plump,
   ready to fall
And burst
   on the ground.

My tongue is dripping
   and I must taste them
Before another moment
   passes.

Jump,
   jump!
Jump!
   Higher, higher!

I'll run and jump,
   with all my might,
To get those grapes
   so high.

Those grapes are
   really up there,
Far beyond
   my reach.

Well, I'll not waste
   another thought on them.
They must be
   very sour!

Land of Aesop – I

Part II

The Goose and the Golden Eggs

There was a farmer who raised a goose. She looked like any other goose.

But when she was old enough to nest, the farmer found her first egg was bright yellow. "How beautiful!" he said, as he held it up and saw it glisten in the sun.

Each day he found his goose had laid another shiny egg, and he would smile.

He soon discovered that these eggs were made of *gold*, and took them to the market where he sold his grain. The people quickly bought every egg he would bring.

Then one day as the farmer was counting his money he said, "I'm getting rich, but not fast enough."

An idea came to him: If I kill the goose and open it up, I can have all the eggs at once. And I will be the richest person of all!

That was exactly what he did—he killed the goose. But when he opened her up he found no eggs! And his precious goose was gone, never to lay another egg.

What can we learn from this?

By wanting too much,
too fast,
You may do something
wrong and lose
what you have.

42

She was a wonderful goose.
  She laid a golden egg
At the start
  of each new day.

The farmer was
  glad to have her,
And by selling the eggs
  he grew more and more rich.

Now the goose was faithful, and
  every morning she'd lay
Another egg, until one afternoon
  her owner became impatient.

He thought,
  What if, instead of only
One gold egg each day,
  I get them all right now?

Well, the goose could lay
  only one new egg each day;
And the farmer lost forever
  the goose and her golden eggs.

43

The Fox and the Crow

One sunny morning a fox went out
in search of something to eat. As he
walked along, his nose began to twitch
at the smell of delicious cheese.

His mouth watered as he sniffed and
then he looked up. There on the branch
of a tree he saw Sally Crow holding a
piece of cheese in her beak.

My search is over, thought the fox.
Now there is my breakfast!

He trotted up to the tree and said
to the crow, "Good morning, beautiful
creature!"

44

But Sally just stood there, cocked her
head and looked. She held the cheese
tightly in her beak, not wanting to drop
her treat.

"How magnificant you look," said
the fox. "How shiny your feathers!
You must have a beautiful voice. If
you would sing, I'd praise you as
Queen of Birds."

Sally soon forgot to be careful.
She would very much like to be called
Queen of Birds. Her mouth opened
wide, and she made the loudest caw a
crow could make. Down fell the cheese,
right into the fox's mouth!

"Thank you," said the fox.

Then as he turned to go he said,
"You certainly have a strong voice, but
you need to be more careful."

What does this tell us about
some people who say nice things?

A person who says
something nice
may be trying to get
Something from the person
who will listen.

When a stranger says
something nice to you, it is
polite to say, "Thank you."
But be careful. This person
may be saying what he
doesn't mean.

Mmmmmm.
   Smell that cheese!
Where could it be,
   just waiting for me?

There it is! Way up high
   in the beak of Sally Crow.
She's so vain—certainly
   not as clever as I!

"Dear Sally,
   you look so nice today!
What have you done
   to make this morning so bright?

"Why, if you would sing,
   I'd call you Queen of Birds.
I know I'd lose my breath
   in the wonder of your voice!"

"Caaaaaaw—Caaaaaaaaw."
   There she goes!
Such a loud and raspy sound
   offends my sensitive ears!

But it's worth the noise
   for the tasty prize.
Here it comes.
   Mmm, mmm!

"Thank you, Sally.
   You are so nice
To share such treats
   with a sly old fox like me!"

The Lion and the Mouse

One day a mouse was walking through the grass. He came upon a sleeping lion he didn't know was there.

He was so surprised that he ran over the lion's nose as he hurried to get away.

The lion awakened, feeling little feet upon his muzzle. He opened his eyes, and in a flash he caught the little mouse under his mighty paw.

"Oh, please, please spare me," begged the mouse. "Let me go and someday I'll repay you."

The lion laughed as he thought, What could a little mouse ever do for me? But with a feeling of kindness, the lion let him go.

Later the lion stood and stretched. Then, as he took a step, he heard a loud snap and suddenly was caught in a net of ropes.

No matter how hard he tried, his powerful paws could not break through. The lion became angry and roared loudly, but all the while the ropes still held him captive.

The mouse heard the lion's voice and hurried over. Then he saw him, the lion who had let him go, now caught in a hunter's net.

This is an easy problem, thought the mouse, and fun too!

He went straight to the ropes and began to chew. Soon he had gnawed through them, and the lion walked out free.

"You laughed when I said I would repay you," said the mouse. "And now, you see—I have!"

What lesson can we learn?

A kind deed is
never wasted.

It pays to be kind:
First, because we help someone.
Then, because that person
    may some day help us,
    or someone else who needs it.

This tall grass tickles
   my nose and whiskers,
And hides me
   as I go.

Oops! No! A lion!
   I must get away.
I didn't see him
   sleeping there.

Now I've done it,
   clumsy me.
I ran
   right over his nose!

Oh, no!
   I'm caught
Under his
   great soft paw!

"Dear Mr. Lion,
   Great King of Beasts,
Please spare me
   and I'll come back.

"I'll come and help you
   when you need it —
You won't be sorry
   you let me go."

The lion is laughing
   at such an idea.
"Do you think YOU
   could help ME?"

He must feel
   kindly today.
He has lifted his paw;
   I'm free to go!

What's that I hear?
   It's the lion's roar!
And he doesn't sound
   very happy.

Where is he? There,
   trapped in a hunter's net.
Aha, now that's
   my specialty!

Quick—I'll gnaw the ropes
   with my sharp little teeth.
See, the net just
   falls away.

"You've freed me!
   Thank you,"
Says the lion, who
   now is my friend.

The Fox Without a Tail

One day a fox caught his tail in the jaws of a steel trap. He tugged and tugged and finally got away. But he had to leave his beautiful tail in the trap.

For many days the fox stayed in hiding. He was too ashamed to let the other foxes see him. He didn't want them to laugh and make fun because he had no tail. Besides, he had been so proud of his tail and liked to show it off.

Then the fox thought of a plan. He called the other foxes to a meeting. He said he had something important to tell them.

When all the foxes had come together, he sat up and made a long speech. He talked about foxes who came to serious misfortune because of the problem of having a tail.

He told of a fox who couldn't outrun pursuing hounds because *the weight of his tail slowed him down.* He told about another fox who was caught by hounds when *his tail got caught in a bush.*

He ended his examples by saying that *people hunt foxes mainly for their tails,* which they cut off as prizes after the hunt.

The fox thought he had given proof that tails are dangerous and useless. He finished his great speech telling the other foxes that it would be best for them to cut off their tails immediately if they believed in life and safety.

As the foxes looked at each other to see what others were thinking, one wise old fox stood up and said, "You speak very well, but turn around and you'll find your answer behind you."

The fox without a tail turned around and suddenly the other foxes began to laugh. Then he knew there was nothing he could say that would convince them to cut off their tails.

If you were one of the foxes at the meeting, and you still had your tail, what could you learn from the wise old fox?

Do not listen to advice
from someone who wants
to bring you down
to where he is.

Here was a fox with a problem—he had no tail. He was clever enough to think of fine-sounding reasons for the others not to have tails.

But they were clever foxes too, and there were many of them at the meeting. Their tails were safe because of the wisdom of the old fox.

How embarrassing
    for a fox like me
To walk around
    without a tail!

I want to hide
    but I can't
Stay out of sight
    forever.

I must go back
    to be with my friends;
But how can I
    without a tail?

Now, I'm a fox—I'm smart.
    I'm very smart.
And I've just thought
    of a plan.

"Friend foxes,
    don't you see
The trouble your tails
    might bring?"

"Ho, ho, turn around,"
    says a wise old fox,
"Your answer
    is behind you."

Well, at least I tried,
    but I cannot fool them.
How can a fox
    outsmart a fox?

The Gnat and the Bull

One hot day a gnat was flying over a meadow. He made a loud buzzing sound for so small a creature.

The gnat began to feel tired. As he looked around for a place to rest, he saw a bull eating grass. He flew over and landed on the tip of one of the bull's horns.

When he was ready to leave, he said, "Mr. Bull, please pardon me for resting on your horn. You must be happy to see me go."

"It doesn't matter to me," said the bull. "I didn't notice you were there."

What can we learn from this story about the gnat and the bull?

We sometimes think
we are more important
than others think we are.

SOMETIMES we think we are
more important than we are.

THEN sometimes we don't feel
as important as we should.

BUT we are all important and
worthy of respect.

I'm such a fine gnat
    in great flying form.
I'll buzz around this meadow
    in full morning glory.

I'm getting tired now
    and I think I'll rest
On that bull over there,
    on his long, pointed horn.

I'm ready to leave—
    let all the world watch!
"Excuse me, Mr. Bull.
    You must be relieved
        to see me go."

"Why, no,"
    says the bull,
"I didn't notice you at all."

Two Travelers and a Bear

Two boys, Tim and John, were walking through the woods. Suddenly a bear came out through some bushes.

Tim was fast and quickly climbed a tree.

John stood frozen and lost his chance to run away. He knew he couldn't fight the bear alone. So he fell to the ground and pretended to be dead. He had heard that bears usually won't touch a dead body.

The bear did as John had hoped. He strolled over, sniffed around John's head for a while, and then walked away.

When it seemed safe, John sat up. His friend, Tim, climbed down the tree and came to him.

"From the tree it looked like the bear was whispering in your ear," said Tim. "What did he tell you?"

John replied with a little smile, "He told me not to walk with someone who would leave his friend in danger!"

What lesson can we learn?

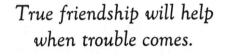

*True friendship will help
when trouble comes.*

Tim was happy to see the bear
only sniff at his friend, John, then
walk away.

Later John saw his chance to say,
in fun, that friends are supposed to
help each other when trouble comes.

Crash go the bushes,
    just to our right.
"A bear!" I cry, and my friend,
    Tim, soon is up a tree.

No time to run
    and certainly
I can't fight this bear
    alone.

I know what I'll do.
    I'll play dead.
I've heard that bears
    don't touch dead things.

Ooooh, that tickles,
    Mr. Bear!
Your wet breath sends
    shivers down my neck.

I'm glad he's gone.
    I'll sit up now
And look for my friend
    who runs so fast.

"Hello," says Tim.
    "Are you okay?
It looked like that bear was
    telling you a secret!"

"You really want to know?"
    He told me not to walk
With someone who would run
    when his friend is in danger!"

Land of Aesop – II

Part III

The Town Mouse and
the Country Mouse

One day a town mouse named Jennifer went to visit her sister, Susan, who lived in the country. Now Susan lived a simple life, making her home in a thick hedge by a field.

Susan served very plain meals—wheat stalks, roots, and acorns with cold water to drink. Her sister, Jennifer, ate only enough of her food to be polite.

After dinner, Susan listened with excitement as Jennifer talked about the city.

They slept well that night, tucked in a safe place in the hedge. Susan dreamed she was a town mouse living where life was exciting.

The next morning, as Jennifer prepared to leave, she said to her sister, "Come with me for a visit to the city. I'll help you get ready." Susan smiled and accepted. Soon they were packed and on their way.

They reached the city and entered the house where Jennifer lived. Susan could hardly believe how big it was.

On the table were candies, nuts, and delicious cheeses. It was the most wonderful place a mouse could imagine!

But as Susan started to take a nibble, she heard a scratch and meow at the door. Her heart stopped beating for a moment. Then she and Jennifer ran to hide.

They kept very quiet and listened. When they thought it was safe, they crept back to the table, looking all around and listening for danger.

Once more they began to eat. Then a door burst open. In came the servants to put the food away, and the house dog was with them!

Susan and Jennifer ran. Down the table leg they went and through a hole in the wall. They barely escaped and hurried between the wall boards until they came into Jennifer's room.

The sisters were breathing hard as Jennifer whispered, "We're out of danger now."

Susan didn't stop to rest but quickly packed her things. When she was finished she said, "Dear sister, you have many nice things here that I don't have. But I prefer my plain food and simple life in the country. And most of all I like my home in the thicket where I feel peaceful and safe."

As Susan started to leave, she stopped for a moment and said, "Please come and visit—any time."

What did Susan, the country mouse, want the most?

Peace and Security

Susan treasured having
a few things in a safe place,
more than many things in
a place where she would
feel afraid, not knowing
what would happen next.

Jennifer's coming.
   I must tidy up.
I wonder what news
   she'll bring from the city.

"Hello, Sister Jennifer."
   "Hello, Sister Susan.
It's so good to be out
   in the fresh country air."

"Come in, Jennifer;
   let's sit down to eat.
The food is quite simple
   but it's certainly healthy."

"Yes, dear sister, I know
   how resourceful you are.
Now, I'll take just a little—
   and thank you so much."

With supper soon ended,
   they talked of the town;
Jennifer told Susan
   the most marvelous things.

"Do come for a visit;
   You'll have a good time."
"Why, thank you for asking.
   Yes—yes, I will come."

The sisters arrived and
   the city was bustling
With sounds of much traffic
   and dogs that were barking.

"Now this is my house
   with many great rooms;
And this is the table,
   all loaded with treats!"

"Jennifer! A cat!
   It's scratching the door.
What a terrible meow.
   It'll be in any second!"

Quickly they ran
   through a hole and hid.
Quietly they waited
   'til the cat went away.

Then back to the food
   with mouths all watering—
"No! Here come the servants
   to clear off the table."

"Run, Susan—
   quick, run and hide.
And watch out for the big dog
   who follows behind."

"Sister Jennifer, I really like
   your mansion so fair,
With its many fine rooms
   and food fit for a king."

"But, Jennifer, dear Jennifer,
   I really must go.
My country home's waiting
   quite snug in its thicket."

The Fox and the Stork

One day a fox named Fred looked over at Bernie Stork. What a funny looking creature, he thought.

I know what I'll do. I'll play a trick on him.

Fred Fox acted very nice and asked Bernie to come over for dinner. "I'm making soup today. I'm sure you will like it."

Bernie accepted the invitation. That afternoon he came over to Fred's place with a good appetite.

"Here it is," said Fred, pouring his homemade soup into plates that were wide and shallow. "My best soup ever! Let's enjoy it."

Now Bernie could only wet the tip of his bill. He thought, I can't enjoy this, one drop at a time. Hmmm . . . I know what I'll do.

"Fred, your soup smells quite good. Come over to visit me tomorrow. I'm making a special fish dinner."

Fred accepted. The next afternoon he came to the river where Bernie lived. He was hungrier than Bernie had been the day before.

"Here it is," said Bernie cheerfully, "served in my nicest jars."

The jars were so tall and narrow that Fred could not reach even one small piece of fish!

Bernie used his long bill to eat all he had put into his jar. He told Fred— between bites—how good it was.

What does this story tell us?

Some people think
one good trick
deserves another.

Be careful how you trick—
  or make fun of someone.
You may find that they
  can trick back in a way
  you won't like.
It is safer not to play tricks
  at all.

Bernie is a silly-looking stork,
 thought Fred, the crafty fox—
Such skinny legs, fat body
 and a long, long bill.

Bernie is not as sleek
 and handsome as I am.
I know what I'll do—
 I'll play a trick on him.

"Hello, Bernie.
 How are you today?
Come over for supper.
 Soup's on and it's good."

Why soup on a plate?
 thought Bernie.
I can only wet
 the tip of my bill!

That Fred
 thinks he's
So wise
 and clever.

"Fred, you must come
 for a visit and eat.
Tomorrow I'm making
 a special fish dinner.

"Welcome, sly Fred,
 you're in time for a treat.
Now here's a great meal
 in my favorite jars.

"It's all that I have
 to serve in, you see.
It fits my long bill, and . . .
 mmmmm—how delicious!"

The Two Pots

Two pots, one made of brass, the other of clay, stood on the hearth of an old fireplace.

One day the brass pot said to the clay pot, "Let's go for a walk."

"I'd rather not," said the clay pot. He went on to explain, "Just a small bump might break me."

"Don't let that keep you from going," said the brass pot. "If anything comes along that could hurt you, I'll step in between and protect you." So the clay pot agreed to go.

Now each pot had but three short legs, and walking made them sway from side to side. With every step they came close to bumping each other.

The clay pot could not go on this way for long. After they had walked a short distance, the two pots did bump, and the clay pot cracked.

"Oh, no!" cried the clay pot. "You had better go on without me." And as he turned to leave, he said, "Instead of protecting me, you easily hurt me!"

What lesson does this teach?

Those with much
in common
make best friends.

Make close friends with
those who have interests and
values similar to yours.

If you don't, you may be
hurt by someone who doesn't
mean to harm you.

Remember also, that you
may be friendly to everyone,
no matter how different each
may be. Every person has a
purpose and all may live and
work in the same world.

There were two pots
  in an old stone house,
And they were
  quite different.

The brass pot was bright
  and kept very shiny
Doing jobs that
  clanged and banged.

The clay pot was filled
  to the brim every day;
It stood by the stove
  and held extra water.

"Take a walk?" said the clay pot
  in shock and dismay.
"No, you're made of strong brass
  and I'm fragile clay."

"Oh, come,"
  said the brass pot.
"Let's walk and
  I'll guard you."

The clay pot went,
  But the two swayed
As they walked,
  and there was a terrible bump.

The clay pot looked
  and to his surprise
Saw cracks running down
  both of his sides!

With this hurt from
  their difference
The walk
  was soon ended.

Unequals may work
  in the same place together
Where each has a job
  that's important and needed.

But when it comes to
  close friendship
It's usually better
  to have much in common.

The Young Goat
and the Wolf

One day, before some shepherds took
their sheep out to pasture, they put a
young goat on the roof of the shelter to
keep him from harm.

When they were gone, the young goat
was curious and began to explore. He
walked to the edge of the roof, and as he
looked down he saw a wolf passing by.

It was safe on the roof and he began
to laugh and make fun of the wolf.

The wolf stayed calm and said to the goat, "I hear you, but I'm not angry with you."

The goat stopped to listen as he heard the wolf speaking:

"Young goat, when you are up there, it is the high roof talking and not you."

Then the wolf turned and walked away.

What lesson can the young goat learn?

Don't say anything
you wouldn't say
anywhere
at any time.

What fun
  to be up
On the roof of
  the shelter.

While everyone is away
  I'll explore
And see what
  I can see.

Look at that wolf,
  so strong and scary!
But I'm not afraid
  here out of his reach.

"Mr. Wolf!
  Mr. Wolf!
I see you—
  I see you!"

"Who's afraid of
  the big bad wolf?
Not me, not me—
  not me-e-e-e!"

"I don't hear you,"
  said the wolf.
"I only hear
  the high roof talking."

And he turned
  and walked away,
Leaving the goat
  by himself.

The goat was brave
  on roofs so high,
But on the ground it
  would be another matter.

The Boy and the Candies

Jack and his mother were visiting
Aunt Mona. Aunt Mona gave him
permission to take some candies from
a pitcher.

Eagerly Jack reached in. He took
so much that he couldn't pull his
hand back out.

He stood there with his fingers
squeezed tightly around as many
candies as he could hold.

Jack wouldn't let a single one go.
And he became upset because no matter
how hard he tried, he couldn't pull his
hand out of the pitcher.

"Jack," said his mother, "be satisfied
to take half as many. Then you'll be able
to pull your hand out. And maybe later
you'll be offered more."

What does this teach us?

Do not reach for
too much at a time.

If you are polite and
take a small amount,
You might be offered more.

I love to eat
   candy.
I can't get
   enough.

"Thank you, Aunt Mona."
   I'll reach right in
And take the biggest handful
   I can hold.

Now my hand is stuck!
   No matter how hard I pull,
I can't get it out
   and I won't let go!

I love these candies
   so much that
I don't want to drop
   even one.

The Rooster and the Jewel

One day, Robby Rooster was busy scratching in the barnyard looking for corn. He liked corn and was pleased whenever he found a kernel.

Robby saw something sparkle in the dust. After a few scratches he discovered it was a jewel someone had lost.

Looking at it he said, "You may have cost very much and the person who lost you would pay much to find you. But for me, I would choose one kernel of corn over all the jewels in the world!"

What does this tell us about the value of things?

Scratch,
   scratch.
I like to
   scratch.

Under the dust
   I find lost corn that
Farmer John drops from
   his old wooden wagon.

I'm not a hen—
   taking time for eggs.
I'm a rooster
   and I like to scratch!

What's that in the dust?
   It's shiny and bright!
Doesn't look like corn
   to me.

It's only a jewel
   that I cannot eat.
I want corn more than
   anything else.

Land of Aesop – III

Type set in 13.5 point Goudy Old Style,
printed on P.H. Glatfelter Co. 60# Thor
paper, alkaline sized acid free, with 50%
recycled fibers.